On Patrol

Written and Lived by: Edward G. Malecki

As Lived and Written by

Edward G. Malecki

Edward G. Malecki

First printing, June, 2008

ISBN 978-0-6152-0986-9
Published by AllawayBooks
www.allawaybooks.com

Printed by Lulu in the United States of America
www.lulu.com

Table of Contents

Foreword

The author Edward G. Malecki joined the Baltimore City Police department shortly after his tour of duty with the Marine Corp. During his employment with the Baltimore City Police Department he attended Essex Community College in pursuit of his Associates Degree in Criminal Justice. While studying he took a creative writing course which prompted him to begin writing about his experiences as a Baltimore City Police Officer.

All of the stories in the book are true even though the names have been changed. The late 60's and early 70's were very tenuous times in Baltimore City and much has been written about the riots and the Black Panthers. Ed worked mostly foot patrol and worked alone which required flexibility and the ability to make quick decisions. This flexibility and attention to detail resulted in his receiving the Medal of Honor which is depicted in one of his stories, "Car 254." Although he was on foot the majority of the time he was responsible for everything from parking tickets to solving homicides. After retiring from the military in 1997, Ed once again took up his much loved hobby of writing and continued to write stories which he now wants to share with anyone interested in the day to day life of a police officer in the late 60's, early 70's.

Joanne Malecki

This book is dedicated to my loving wife Joanne and daughter Shannon who made this book possible by just helping me to make it happen. Thank-You.

Chapter One

Encounter with a Stranger

Encounter With a Stranger

It was a foggy night in the ghetto. There was a fine mist in the air. It sent a chill up and down my spine. It felt like at any moment a *Wolfman* type character would jump out of a doorway. My thoughts were broken by a voice shouting in the dark, "Police! Help, police!"

It sounded like a child's voice. I ran down the street towards the sound. I could see a small figure in the fog. It turned out to be a little boy.

He shouted, "Up the stairs, help!" and ran ahead of me. I had a hard time keeping up with him. He ran into an old house in the 2200 block of Caroline Street. Most of the houses were condemned in this area.

I followed him through the front door and down a long hallway. I found myself stumbling up a flight of winding, creaky stairs. My foot went right through a rotten step, ripping the flesh from my shin. Holding my leg, grunting in pain and cursing under my breath, I watched my flashlight fall down the steps and disappear with a thud.

My imagination began to play tricks. Only then was I aware of the complete darkness. Breathing hard, I tried to hold my breath so that I could hear the faintest sound. *Where was that kid?* There it was, that thumping. I put my hand on my revolver trying to reassure myself. I could barely hear it. Then it dawned on me: I was listening to my own heart beat.

Chuckling nervously, I called out to the boy, "Hello, anyone there?" No response. I knew he was there somewhere. *Was this a set-up? Was I being lured into my own coffin?*

Feeling the walls and steps like a blind man, I slowly worked my way to the second floor. God, this place was dark!

Suddenly, my hand struck a door knob. Listening for the smallest whisper, I put my ear to the door. A blood curdling scream sent hot and cold flashes through my body. The door flung open with a bang and someone or something brushed by me, clattering down the steps. I heard the front door creak open then slam shut. Again, the silence. My skin crawled with goose pimples. I could not stop now. I saw a soft flickering light coming from somewhere in the apartment. I could hear moaning.

Positive this was the stage for my execution, I drew my revolver. I crept into the first room, feeling my way as I went along. A cold splash and rattling of pots and pans assured me that this was the kitchen. My hand was elbow deep in cold greasy dish water.

Getting to the next room, I could hear the roaches' crisp bodies popping under my feet. Now, I could see the flickering light was a small candle. There was enough light to distinguish that this was the bedroom. Hot beads of sweat covered me from head to toe. I experienced myself getting weak and my legs turning to jelly. *God, don't let me pass out!* I wanted to speak, but when I opened my mouth only silence spilled forth. My tongue was stuck to the roof of my mouth.

I breathed in deeply, wanting to fill my lungs with fresh air and pull myself together. But I was greeted instead by a stench that made my stomach turn over. I started to vomit but was able to hold it down.

Then I got lucky, I banged my head into a kerosene lantern hanging from the ceiling. I was getting tired of the *Cops and Robbers* game. Carefully using the candle, I lit the lantern. The room was filthy. Clothes were piled everywhere. A scrub bucket sat next to the bed. I could see why the room smelled so terrible. The bucket was being used as a toilet and hadn't been emptied for at least a week. The window, dressed in torn plastic curtains was closed.

It was then I saw them lying on the bed. She was alive but motionless in a pool of blood. He looked at me with squinting tearful eyes. Saliva ran from his lips. Lips that were distorted and slowly twisting with agony. His skin was tightening as he moved his jaw from side to side, fighting to open his mouth. Tears ran freely down his blue face. I could feel his pain as his naked, blood stained body twisted and jerked.

It was obvious that he was dying. He was choking to death. In his last moments of desperation, he kicked and lashed out for life itself.

I placed my lips on his, holding his nose. I blew vigorously into his mouth. I saw his chest and stomach rise. He began to cough and scream at the top of his lungs.

The room was suddenly filled with flashing lights, blinding me. My vision blurred. I could see people rushing towards me. Someone grabbed me by the shoulders and said, "It's all over."

I never felt so relieved in my life.

That was the first time that I had ever delivered a baby!

Chapter Two

An Experience in Haste

An Experience in Haste

Here I am, a former Marine of six years, including time in Vietnam and presently a sergeant with the Baltimore City police department. I'm six foot tall and two hundred pounds. I've been with the City Fathers for almost ten years now. I've worked in the ghettos and some pretty rough areas. I've functioned in many different police roles and enjoyed the variety. I've had the opportunity to be involved in some very strange cases.

One month's assignment was to chauffer around a newly appointed Lieutenant. I was to familiarize him with all locations and methods of operation in his newly acquired district in the ghetto. In police talk, we summarize those instructions and interpret them as follows. Take the new shavetail lieutenant by the hand. Show him where he can go and keep warm during December and cool in July. By all means, point out several nice places where he can eat a hot meal at least twice a day. Lunch here! Supper there! Five times a week with the cost being next to nothing, on the house. During this little tour, point out the good guys and the bad guys. The junkies, bookies, pimps, and punks. Above all, don't let him get hurt.

Now keep in mind that this particular lieutenant was a short, overweight, middle aged man. He was obviously an only child with masculinity leaning more to his mothers' side than his fathers. As a patrolman and sergeant, he worked in an area referred to by my men as the

"Country Club" where breaking a window was a serious offense.

During our first day on the job, we began our relationship with a clear understanding that he was anxious and eager to learn. He did not object to constructive criticism. I introduced myself as Sergeant John Edwards and told him he could call me Duke. He shook my hand with determination and a feeling of brotherhood and officially introduced himself as Lieutenant Frederick Spon. He told me I could call him Lieutenant Spon.

We were working the 4:00 pm to 12:00 am watch on a quiet Sunday evening. The weather couldn't have been better for June.

I was inside the station house explaining to Freddy (Lieutenant Spon) a few administrative details. It was obvious that he was bored. He muttered under his breath that there was no action, no excitement. This was confirmed by the silence of the station house police monitor.

We sat down to drink a nice, hot cup of coffee. Suddenly, the monitor blared, "Burglary in Progress." Freddy jumped up and rushed to the monitor. Thanks to his excitement, I am now wearing my coffee down the front of my white shirt. I started to curse and give him constructive criticism, but, he excitedly responded with a "Shh" as he waived his hand in my face to keep me quiet. The monitor blared. We could hear the policemen at the scene of the burglary. The burglary was at a liquor store approximately 15 blocks from our station on Edison Highway.

A voice shouted out, "There they go!" BANG! BANG! Two shots rang out. Voices clashed on each others transmissions. Three more shots could be heard. I was so interested I forgot about my coffee soaked shirt.

Then the dreaded call of "Officer Assist! .....Officer is down."

I could hear police sirens wailing and an ambulance in the background. An officer's voice shouting, "Christ, my partner has been hit. Get that damn ambulance over here. They're on the ground!"

Another voice, "In pursuit of two males driving in a 1964 Green Pick-up Truck". Maryland License number 3442 - D David D David. West bound in the 2000 block of Sinclair Lane heading towards Edison Highway." It sounded a little like Vietnam all over again. Gunshots! Sirens! People shouting in the area.

Freddy and I instinctively ran from the station house to his new shiny police vehicle that seemed to be sitting like a racing stallion in the starting gate. I've been through these emergency calls before and this was no time to panic. As concerned as I was, I couldn't help but chuckle when Lieutenant Spon banged his head on the roof of the car as he tried to get in faster than he could duck down. When his white and gold hat fell to the ground I thought he was going to cry.

I peeled away with the rear wheels screaming in pain. My heart was beating fast. My gut tightened up while my eyes were constantly shifting. This iron stallion had the power and I wasn't holding any in reserve. My palms were sweating, making it difficult to drive. *Time. Time. I wish this was a jet engine.* The car radio blared away. I came to a screeching halt at Brendan and Sinclair Lanes. I positioned the car broadside across Sinclair Lane blocking any passage. I advised a dispatcher of the single road block position. I could see the stream of blue lights, like so many lightening bugs in the night. I could see the flashing exchange of gunfire.

Leaning across the trunk, I looked down at the five notches in my pistol grip. Like a gunslinger I had one notch for each man I had shot in past shootouts. Will I make it through this one? I got that familiar feeling of *Could this be the one?*

In a matter of seconds all of the life and death situations I'd ever encountered ran through my mind. Was there any fact to the superstition "One too many?" Cold sweat poured down from my armpits to my legs. Although the weather was warm, I had the chills. *What the hell was I doing here?* I thought of my wife and children.

Just then Freddy slapped me on the back like an old pal. "Here he comes," he said. From the suddenness of his slap, I damn near wet myself. I looked at Lieutenant Spon. He looked like a kid locked out of a boys room and couldn't hold it any longer.

Then it happened! The great calm I call professionalism. It's a feeling of God sitting on my shoulder and taking over. . Snapping out of it, I heard myself shouting, "Don't sweat it Freddy. We've got 'em baby!"

Grabbing the radio mike I requested the speed of the truck. He was now approximately three blocks away. One of the pursuing officers replied, "I'm doing 80 and he's pulling away from me." I knew this guy was going to ram us. *Hell, at that speed, I'll rest in peace all right! A piece of me here, a piece of me there.* I had no intention of letting that ugly truck break up my body. I jumped into the car leaving Lieutenant Spon crouched down behind the parked car. I backed the car up three feet when I saw Lieutenant Spon open fire, shooting at the on coming truck. Freddy fired that six shot revolver so fast it looked like one long bullet coming out of the barrel. He slowed the truck driver down just long enough for me to back out of the way. The truck zoomed past blazing away with seven police cars in hot pursuit. Lieutenant Spon's new shiny police car now had two bullet holes. One in the door. The other in the window.

I was so elated at Freddy's actions and the fact that I had cheated death one more time that I started to laugh. I gave Freddy thumbs up and jumped in the car. He looked at me with tears in his eyes like a father looks at a new born child. Laughing and holding back the tears of relief he called me a crazy bastard. Both of us laughing after a quick handshake, we were two lunatics ready for the funny farm. We roared away and joined the chase.

Edward G. Malecki

Chapter Three

Three Little Pigs

Three Little Pigs

Once upon a time there were three little pigs: Officer Smith, Officer Seal and Sergeant John Edwards. One day while working in the concrete forest of Baltimore City, the first pig received a call to 123 Gay Street, "Man with a Gun".

Turning on his blue emergency light and siren, he responded to the address as fast as the creatures in the forest would let him. Even though the emergency light was flashing and the siren was wailing, many of the forest creatures would not get out of his way.

Arriving at the address, he rushed up and knocked at the front door. The door flung open and there stood a drunken, fat, female hippopotamus. She was naked from the waist up and she was quite a sight to see. Her oversized breasts hung just above her waist. She was all sweaty and her black hair appeared to be an abandoned rat's nest. It was all greasy and slightly gray from dirt. Her mouth was very large and it was plain to see her rotten teeth. When she spoke, the pig had to turn his head so that her stinking breath wouldn't make him vomit. In a loud drunken voice, she greeted the pig, "What the hell took you so long? He's upstairs. Go get him!"

Now the pig has to be very careful not to violate any of the creatures constitutional rights. So as a matter of necessity, he asked the hippo if she called the police. The fat hippo politely belched in his face and the odor was enough to make him gag. She waddled over to the stairs, grabbing the railing to keep from falling on her drunken face and shouted upstairs, "Hit me now you bastard while the cops are here." Officer Smith advised the hippo that by law she had to obtain a warrant. While attempting to gain the necessary information for the police report, he was rudely interrupted by the growl of the mean wolf upstairs. He could hear the wolf thrashing around and breaking things.

Now, the pig had enough probable cause to go upstairs and investigate. Very carefully, he crept up the steps. The thrashing noise stopped. It was very quiet. The pig was scared; his heart beat quickened. Officer Smith was very young. He had only been a pig for two years and had a lot to learn about the creatures of the forest. He thought for sure that the wolf was hiding under the bed. With gun in hand, the pig shouted, "Come out from under the bed!" But the wolf tricked the pig. Very slowly, the wolf slipped out of a clothes closet. The hippo downstairs kept shouting and calling the wolf one dirty bastard after another. With all that noise it was difficult for the pig to listen for the wolf. The wolf snuck up behind the pig and said in a very deep voice, "Hey Pig."

The startled pig turned around. He saw a bright flash and heard a loud boom. He felt himself being hurled through the air landing in the corner of the room. He felt a burning, empty feeling in his stomach and the hammer of hell beating on his groin. In his semi-conscious condition, he realized that his stomach and groin had been blown apart. The wolf had used a sawed off 12 gauge shot gun at point blank range on him.

The second pig, Officer Seal burst through the front door. The wolf, now standing at the top of the stairs shouted, "Come and get yours Pig." Two quick shots rang out from Seal's revolver. The wolf spun around in pain. The top section of his left shoulder was torn away. Flesh and blood splattered everywhere. The wolf fell down the steps and lay at Officer Seal's feet screaming in pain.

Officer Seal bent over to pick up the wolf's shot gun and didn't pay much attention to the hippo. All of this excitement frightened the hippo. Seeing her mate covered with blood and screaming caused her mothering instincts to ooze out of her. In deep concern and fear for her mate's life, the hippo produced a nine inch butcher knife. With tremendous power she drove the knife through the side of Officer Seals face into the right cheek and out the left side. The pig's mouth fell open and his tongue toppled to the floor like a piece of fresh liver.

The third pig, Sergeant John Edwards entered the house just in time to see Officer Seal fall on his face as he reached out in agony for the fat hippo. Pigs were pouring through the front door. There were many creatures of the forest watching the pigs as they placed the hippo in the cruising patrol paddy wagon and the wolf in the ambulance. The hippo shouted to the wolf, "I love you darling!" As the black morgue wagon drove away with the two dead pigs you could hear strange sounds coming from within the

crowd   of   creatures.   OINK,
Oink...Oink....Oink

Chapter Four

Call My Bluff

Call My Bluff

Hi, my name is John Edwards. My friends call me Duke. I've been in uniform patrol for nine years. During those nine years I've learned a lot from the older guys.

There are some things you keep your mouth shut about and then there are the things you bitch about. Knowing the difference can either get you killed or save your life. Today was a great day for me. I was asked to join the tactical unit. This was quite a step up in my career.

The TAC unit only consisted of four patrolmen and one sergeant. The sergeant answered directly to the district commander who was a captain. We answered only to the sergeant.

It was a pretty tight ship. The senior TAC guys were Lenny Santo and Bob Jacobs. Both men have been in TAC as long as I could remember. I've seen numerous guys come and go but these two were extremely tight with the sergeant. Lenny was a lay-back type but very street smart. He was a lot like the sergeant. He never said much but when he did you listened. Bob on the other hand was a sheep. If Lenny came to a sudden stop Bob's head would go up Lenny's ass. Bob never impressed me much and I wondered how in the hell he got where he was. Bottom line, they were the senior TACS and we were just lucky to be there.

I found out later that Lenny and Bob were in the navy together and that Bob had an uncle who was a district commander. Well that solved the mystery of how Bob got there.

What was unique about TAC was that you worked in plain clothes but you were not a detective. You were called a tactical officer. We had to be clean shaved and have a decent hair cut. Our main function was to solve large rings of crime. Like a string of burglaries done by the same group of guys. Or a car theft ring. Lenny favorite was narcotic dealers. He had developed such good Confidential Informants (CI's) over the years it was a walk in the park for those two.

My new partner was a great guy named Willie Boyd. He was a small guy but very smart. He was also hand picked from patrol. He had about five years in uniform and had an old sergeant in patrol that had raised him like a son after his dad died. He had a cheerful personality, two small children and a pretty young wife. We hit it off right from the get go.

Our first assignment was a rash of burglaries in a concentrated area. Well we plotted the burglaries on the map and it was easy to see a pattern. We figured out the time was between nine o'clock and twelve. So we hit the street in the area where the break-ins were taking place. It was a warm summer night, it was dark and all seemed calm. When Willy's pager went off with a 911 call from a CI, we went directly to a phone in the area and returned the call.

I could hear the CI shouting into the phone "Right now he's breaking in. I can see him from here. He's wearing a red jacket, dungarees and a dark bandana around his head. He's a white male in his twenties about 5-9, 185lbs. He's leaving now."

I was standing next to Willy under the street light when all of a sudden here comes the son of bitch. He was running by me. He fit the description to a tee. He was shitting and getting. All I said to Willy was, "I got him," and I took off running. I chased him across the street and down a back alley. It was a good thing I wore my tennis shoes that night. I was gaining. The back alley in this part of the ghetto was bad. Trash, old couches, chairs, and mattresses paved my way down the alley. I managed to stay three feet behind him. Gasping for air, and breathing like a race horse, my heart was beating like a drum. We had run about a city block at full out speed. I was running out of juice. The adrenaline was there but my legs started to turn to rubber.

It was hard to breathe. Now I wasn't sure if this guy had done a felony Burglary or a misdemeanor breaking and entering. There is a big different here when you talk probable cause. Well I just said *fuck it*, pulled out my snub nose 38 caliber revolver, got shoulder to shoulder with the guy and said, "Stop or I'll shoot."

I pointed the gun directly at his head. I could hardly get the words out I was so tired. Well I made my play but he wasn't buying it. He just shouted back. "Shoot me motherfucker."

I still wasn't sure of the probable cause. We were still shoulder to shoulder when I saw it in the moonlight. It was a big old wheelbarrow. It was just sitting there ahead of us. I waited until we got almost on top of it when I pushed him into it. He hit that son of bitch like a ton of bricks and fell to the ground. After rolling around on the ground he just stopped and came to a sitting position. My chest was heaving and was soaking wet from sweat. When I stopped and went over to him the bastard wasn't even breathing hard. I reached down with what little strength I had left and went to grab him by the shoulder and say, "You're under arrest."

Before I could say arrest, he grabbed my arm, stood up, and flipped me over his shoulder and proceeded to punch my lights out. We rolled in filthy standing water exchanging punches when he made the fatal mistake of putting his hands on my gun which I had in my right hand. I squeezed the trigger knowing the side blast would burn his hand and make him let go or maybe shoot off one of his fucking fingers. I fired one shot it worked. He tried again and I fired another shot and he let go. It was clear at this point that he wanted to shoot me with my own gun.

Now I definitely had probable cause for a felony charge. He continued to whale on me. I was so tired but I wasn't letting this bastard go.

Finally I said to him, "you want this fucking gun so bad, you can have it, but bullets first. " I placed the gun directly on his left knee cap and squeezed the trigger. "Oh, you cocksucker," he said, "You shot me." He started to punch me in the face. I was running on pure adrenaline. Enough was enough.

I jammed that snub nose right into his face, cocked the hammer, and shouted out, "Now fucker, call my bluff." I could hear the sirens of the marked units trying to find us. I lay there next to him for what seemed like an hour when I finally had the strength to get on my feet. He started to get up and was in a bent over position when I dropped kicked him in the face. He fell to the ground when I looked out the corner of my eye I could see a uniform policeman standing there. It was clear that the uniform police was a young black rookie. I figured he saw me kick the guy and was ready to charge me with brutality.

I turned to him and said "The son of a bitch tried to shoot me with my own gun." All he said to me was, "Are you alright officer?" as he patted me on the shoulder. Bleeding from the nose and mouth, and covered with the filth from the alley, I hooked up with Willy. We were going to put this guy away for a long time.

It was now about 1 o'clock in the morning and I couldn't wait to get home, get cleaned up and be ready for court at nine o'clock in the morning.

After having great nights sleep I went to the station house to get my prisoner for court. My prisoner was sitting in the office with Lenny and Bob. I said, "What the fuck is going on?"

Lenny replied, "This prisoner is ours by order of the TAC sergeant. "

That prick sat there with a cast on his knee and a smirk on his face as he spilled his guts about the rash of burglaries. It was clear that the senior TACS were going to make this guy a CI, in exchange for information and my charges would turn to shit. Well I learned my lesson that day.

Edward G. Malecki

Chapter Five

Misfire

Misfire

Willy and I have been working together now for about two months. Things couldn't be better. We were doing quite well solving cases. Of course we avoided Lenny and Bob whenever we could. Our CI list was growing and growing. Lenny would ask, "How are you guys doing?" We would reply, "Hanging in there."

We stopped taken our CI's to the office so Lenny didn't know who they were. It worked out quite well. There had been a rash of store burglaries in our area. The TAC sergeant decided to put us on patrol in an unmarked unit you could spot a mile away with the big spot on the door. We worked the four to twelve shifts. I didn't mind it as long as we got out of the office.

It was summer time and about nine thirty. The sun had gone down and it was getting dark. As we patrolled the area I would flash our spotlight on the store windows and doors. It seemed pretty boring and then I spotted something strange. I shined my light on the storefront window which was about six feet by six feet and I got a glare back from the glass which was good, but when I shined the light on the side area I received nothing. This told me the glass was missing. Willy and I bailed out of the car.

It was an automatic response. I took the front and Willy took the back. I looked through the front but it was too dark. I couldn't see anything.

Then came that gut feeling like, *Do I have to go in? Well of course I have to go in!* So I squeezed through the open window onto a two foot ledge in the store front. I got inside and jumped off the two foot ledge to the floor. I didn't like this a little bit. With my 38 snub nose in one hand and flashlight in the other I took one step forward. It was really dark. Cold chills started running up my back. *What the hell am I doing here? Why didn't I just call for a marked unit to back us up and then go in?* Well it was a little too late to second guess myself. I didn't want to turn my flashlight on for fear of giving someone a perfect target. I stood there in the dark waiting and listening. I held my breath so I could hear the faintest sound, only to hear my heart pounding. There was that sixth sense that told me not to move. I blinked my eyes rapidly in an attempt to focus in the dark. Then I saw him.

He was a tall dark shadow hiding behind the counter. I shouted out, "Police, come out with your hands up."

No response. I knew Willy was in the back and had no idea what was going on. *Another fuck up in communication.* I kept blinking my eyes trying to see better in the dark. Finally I held the flashlight away from my body and turned it on. I could clearly see the black male in his twenties covered with sweat crouched behind the store counter. I was really leery about this guy. I could see his hands were empty but he was scared to death. And he didn't want to move. I didn't want to call for Willy for fear it might spook this guy.

Finally, I pulled the old bluff and shouted, "Come out from there or I'll blow you away." You can't just shoot people because you're scared.

Well it worked. I heard him say, "I give up officer." With that he stepped forward. I put the flashlight in my pocket and grabbed him by the back of his belt and pants with my left hand. We started to leave the store through the open window. That was a big mistake. I could feel the adrenaline pumping through this guy but I wasn't going to let him go. It was like walking on egg shells. Waiting for the next move.

It all happened so quickly. I'm holding onto this guy by his back pants with my gun in my right hand. As we stepped up onto the two foot ledge he crashed right through the six by six foot window. How in gods name we never got cut I don't know. He jumped to the pavement with me hanging on to him. As a result of him twisting when he hit the side walk he flipped me on to my back. In a flash he had both hands on my revolver.

Cold sweat pumped over me as I wondered where the hell Willy was. My left hand was twisted in his back pants. I couldn't get it free. This sucker was strong. He grabbed my pistol in my right hand and stuck it into my mouth.

I franticly moved my trigger up and down in the trigger guard to keep him from getting his finger in there, too late, the hammer fell and I pissed myself.

Misfire. The son of a bitch didn't go off. All I could figure was that my thumb hit the hammer just enough to slow down the strike of the firing pin. I was totally drained. My chest was heaving as I gasped for air. Then I saw an arm go around his fucking neck and jerk him upward. It was Willy.

Still lying on my back and covered in glass I told Willy to hold him there as I drove my right fist straight up into his mouth. It wasn't the smartest thing to do. His front tooth came out and lodged between my knuckles. But I did feel better.

We charged him with burglary, assault on a police officer, resisting arrest, and attempted murder of a police officer. He got fifteen years. I thanked Willy for being there for me and we went to the hospital to get my hand fixed. Well they took out the tooth, bandaged my hand and gave me a tetanus shot.

The TAC sergeant was pleased but gave me hell for not calling for backup. So many atta boys and one ah shit. Well that's not the end of the story. I worked for about week with the bandaged hand when it started to thump. It was was hurting pretty bad. I told Willy that I better get it checked. Off to the hospital we went. I no sooner sat down in the emergency room when they told me I was to be admitted immediately for blood poisoning. I didn't realize it, until they showed me the dark blue line going up my arm.

After I was admitted I had an intravenous injections in one arm and my right arm was propped up in a sling. They said it had to drain. Well at this point I really didn't think much about it until the doctor came into my room and started to draw blue lines on my knuckles. He advised me that if it didn't drain within the next twelve hours he would have to cut off my two middle fingers. He further advised me if the poison didn't stop it would reach my heart and that I would die. Now I'm not a religious person but that night I was reborn. I couldn't sleep. I lay there in a pool of sweat, asking myself *Why I had to pick out the dirtiest mouth and punch him...*

I swore I would never hit another person in the mouth again. I also swore that I would never rush into a situation like that without calling for back up. I swore a lot of things that night. Come morning I was still wide awake.

When the doctor told me all went well and that the poison had drained out I was so happy I started to cry. With joy. The boss gave me a couple of days off then it was back to work as usual.

Chapter Six

The Alamo Stand-off

The Alamo Stand Off

Willy and I decided to take a break and we were hungry. The best place to eat was Finnegan's Café and Tavern. It was located on the very end of the Harford Road strip. The strip consisted of taverns, pawn shops, and pool halls. Finnegan's was the only white bar left. I knew the owner quite well and felt safe in his place. His cook, Miss Miller, made the best chili around and it was free to the police. It was getting pretty late.

It was about nine o'clock. Willy and I entered the café and found it to be empty. Just the way we liked it. It had a long bar and at the end was the chili. Mike the owner was behind the bar. He was a big man with a great sense of humor. "Come on in," he shouted, as we entered the bar. "The chili is still hot. How are you guys doing? It's a slow night for me too."

We all laughed as Willy and I sat at the far end of the bar near the back door but facing the front door. We sat there for about ten minutes enjoying our chili. Mike was glad to have us around for protection and we knew it. That's why the chili was free to police as long as you ate it there. The bar was dimly lit.

We were enjoying our free meal when the front door swung open. A thin black male about nineteen entered the bar, walked to the center of the bar and requested a bag of potato chips. We didn't think much of it, but it was clear the guy was very nervous and kept looking around like he expected more people. He got his chips and left through the front door. It wasn't five minutes later another skinny black male about twenty entered through the front door and did the same thing. He walked to the center of the bar and requested a bag of potato chips. Now this guy really looked nervous. He got his chips and left.

By this time Willy and I smelled a rat. We told Mike to stay behind the bar while we went outside to check out the situation. Now keep in mind, Willy and I were working plainclothes at the time. We opened the front door and walked about eight feet when we saw four black males get out of a black late model Ford.

They stood shoulder to shoulder under the street light. It was clear to see all of them had a pistol. Willy and I stood next to each other, drew our pistols, and I shouted, "Police, Freeze."

This time I got on my walkie-talkie and requested a 10-13, Officer needs assistance, call. I gave out our location but my voice was very calm and quiet. I didn't want to spook these guys. I guess the dispatcher didn't believe me because he came back with, "Are you having a problem?"

I replied, "We have our two pistols drawn and they have their four pistols out. It looks something like the Alamo."

We all just stood there frozen in time looking at each other with our guns drawn. It seemed like everything went in slow motion. The silence was broken when I shouted out again, "Police put down your guns."

Three guys dropped their guns on the street but the fourth guy shouted out, "Fuck you," and pointed his weapon at us.

He raised his weapon and I squeezed the trigger on my gun. I was now sporting a brand new 45 caliber colt automatic pistol. It sounded like a cannon going off as the round ripped through his left shoulder and tore out the back of his shoulder spinning him around and knocking him to the ground. Now a 38 cal would have never have done that. The three males raised their hands and surrendered.

Willy covered the prisoners as I went for the driver who was behind the wheel of the Ford. He was trying to pull something from his right coat pocket but it got hung up. I stuck my 45 in his face and said "Forget it asshole," He threw up his hands and I recovered a 357 magnum from his coat pocket.

By this time marked units with their bright lights were all over the place.

Willy and I arrested all five subjects and charged them with possession of a deadly weapon and assault for the guy I shot. It was obvious they were going to hold up the bar, but we couldn't prove it.

Further examination of the black Ford revealed numerous bullet holes in the rear trunk. Willy and I felt good about the arrest. We could get these guys for a string of hold ups. Well, did I speak too soon? We no sooner got to the station when we were told that Lenny and Bob would take over the case.

I was really getting tired of this shit. We do all the work and Lenny and the asshole get all the credit. Well at least my shot was called a good shoot. Willy and I remained together for another six months as close partners in a tactical unit. Then one day Willy was transferred to a cream of the crop position, Homicide. He was a good cop and I'm sure his uncle helped him get transferred.

I didn't want to break in a new partner so I went back into uniform patrol. Well I now work the Harford Road Straight- a -way and continue to dine at Finnegan's.

Chapter Seven

Surrender, or Die

Surrender or Die

It was a warm July day. Ten o'clock in the morning and it was already 70 degrees.

We were gathered for our squad meeting at the station house. We had a special unit. It was called Area Three Narcotics Squad and was made up of six handpicked men. All six of us went to a special eight week school on narcotics. It was a really informative school. We learned how to identify just about every drug you could name or at least what was on the street, how to make it, grow it, smoke it, shoot it and most of all how to fake it.

Then came the paper work, we knew more about probable cause and how to do search warrants then most attorneys. We had daily drills on search and seizures. By the time we graduated we felt like junkies and drug dealers.

There was also a lot of instruction in undercover work. The Area Three stood for three districts in the city. Baltimore city was made up of nine districts. We covered the North East, Southeast and Eastern districts. The northeastern and the southeastern districts were mostly made of Caucasians. The Eastern district was predominately Black.

All three districts had very bad narcotic problems. All we had to do was infiltrate, fit in, make buys, and let the uniform guys for the most part make the arrest.

We always worked in two man teams. I was a little different than the rest of the squad.

I weighed about 220, was 6ft 4 and I'm white. I was 26 yrs old. I drove a Harley motorcycle provided by the department with unlisted plates. At that time I had long shoulder length hair and a full beard. I was to pass myself off as a body guard or hit man. My name was Animal. It worked out pretty well. I would take a confidential informant (CI) and go where ever to make a buy or be there when the dope was being processed. I would pose as a bodyguard for my informant. I carried a 45 Cal pistol and a 12 gauge sawed off shotgun.

My main function was to get the information to make the arrest. Like I said we traveled in pairs. My side partners' job was a little stickier. He would pose as a street dealer or junkie. Everything depended on the CI that he was associated with. I'm sure if they knew that the CI was an undercover informant they would kill all three of us.

It was quite clear to see why we were very careful in who we picked as a CI. You have to be careful that the CI doesn't work both sides of the fence. A lot of it depended upon your gut feeling.

As for my partner his name was String. I couldn't have picked a better sidekick. String was 24 years old, weighed in at about 145 soaking wet. He had long blond hair, a bad set of teeth and for some reason had black circles under his eyes. I used to tell him he looked like death warmed over.

He would just smile, show those bad teeth and reply, "That look is what keeps me alive." He was really quite fit. I've seen him in a couple of scrapes. He was very fast and wiry. He had two years of college and had majored in, can you believe it, ACTING.

Then there was Murphy. He was your average Joe. Clean cut, in his early 20's, but he sported a manicured beard and pony tail. He was your typical street dealer. The other three guys were made up of the same chemistry: Bodyguard, street dealer, and junkie.

We've been on the street for about nine months and had quite an arrest record. We were really getting in with the big boys, that being organized crime. In our travels we ran into several DEA [Drug Enforcement Agency] government undercover agents. These guys were really good and hooked us up with some heavy players.

We met one of our CI's at the airport who gave us a great tip about an arrival. The guy walked off the plane from Turkey with two open shopping bags full of hashish and one pound of cocaine. In those days no one really knew too much about drugs. This guy turned out to be quite a nice person and a very valuable to us. We made him a CI.

Well anyway here we are having coffee and getting our shit together when another one of our CI's called on my pager. He entered 911. This was hot information. I returned his call and my ears were burning. Turns out there was a Black guy 5-10 medium build, 30ish, 185 lbs, blue shirt and dark pants, driving a 66 Ford, green in color, with Maryland tag GHT 3487.

He was sitting in the bar at Hoffman and Eagle streets at the Hilltop Inn. He had in his possession an 8 x 10 glossy of me and String and had stated that he had been paid to take us out.

I thanked the CI and informed the rest of the squad. Well the adrenaline was pumping so hard you could cut it with a knife. We were familiar with the location and knew an alley that emptied into the street adjacent to the Hilltop Inn. The Hilltop Inn was a tavern. We didn't want to pull up too close to the tavern and bailout of our car without getting positive identification. We wanted to get the guy outside of the bar to see if he would get into the green Ford. I didn't want to shoot a Black male just because he looked like the guy.

The six of us were crouched down in the alley about forty feet from the car when we saw a guy fitting the description get into the Ford. It all happened so fast I don't know if the guy saw us from the tavern or not. He revved the engine and peeled away from the curb. We all ran across the street towards the Ford. Then it happened.

Boom! One blast from the driver's shotgun. I could feel the sting but it really didn't hurt as bad as I expected. The blast bit into my lower right leg. I was bleeding pretty badly as he roared toward me. He was only eight feet from me as I hit the ground and rolled under a parked car. I could hear the metal twist and bend as the Ford smashed into the parked car, in an attempt to run me down. Then he backed up and started down the street again. I couldn't feel anything. The adrenaline was pumping and pumping. I thought my heart would pop out of my chest. I heard the gunfire from the rest of the squad.

As I looked out from under the parked car I could clearly see the two rear tires of the Ford about three feet from me. I took aim and fired two shots. The bullets from my 45 caliber found their mark. Both tires went flat as he slowly wobbled continuing down the street away from me. I slid out just in time to see the Ford hit String head-on.

I couldn't believe it. That skinny bastard jumped onto the front hood of the car, ran over the roof, and rolled down the trunk, and hit the ground in a perfect sitting position. He fired one shot from his

38 cal. The round hit the rear window and slid upwards where it stopped and stuck in the roof of the car. So much for a 38 caliber. He fired five more shots into the trunk to no avail.

The rest of the squad was now running down the street. They were on foot but in hot pursuit.

Then I was feeling the pain. String came over to me and tore off his tee shirt and tied it around my leg. I felt so useless. All I could do was watch as the Ford made a wobbly right turn on the next street with the squad closing in. The streets were now getting full of nosey people all wanting to see the gun fire. By this time marked units started to arrive.

String never left my side. We directed the units to the next block where the Ford had turned.

The rest of the story I got from Murphy, one of the squad members. It seemed that the Ford turned onto the next street and the guy bailed out and ran into a house at 243 Moser Street. Uniformed guys hit the front door as Murphy and the rest of the squad were waiting at the back door. The Black male came running out with his shotgun in hand. Murphy and the rest of the squad politely pointed their weapons at his head and said, "Surrender or die".

The Black male dropped his weapon and threw his hands up into the air. No one else was injured in the operation. The Green Ford was stolen. The black and white 8x 10 photographs of String and I which started this whole thing were recovered. We also recovered a 45 Caliber pistol from the car. The Black male got 20 years for attempted murder of a police officer. He never revealed who paid him to make the hit.

Edward G. Malecki

Chapter Eight

Lucky Lewis

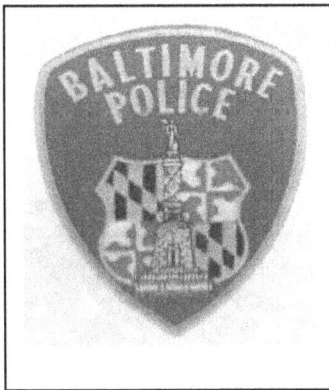

Lucky Lewis

It was a pleasant summer day on June 14, 1968. Me and my two buddies, String and Rabbit jumped into a blue '62 LTD. This baby was like a boat. She ran smooth and had power to spare. String sank into the back seat and crawled into a fetal position. At 5'9 and 145 lbs this was an accomplishment. With his drawn in face and black circles under his eyes he looked like death warmed over. He looked sick but was quite healthy.

Rabbit wasn't much different. He was slightly heavier but had a bad acne problem. He sat next to me in the front seat. As for me, well I was the complete opposite. At 220 lbs and 6'4, you could hardly see my face with the thick full beard and long hair. My friends called me "Animal". I was your typical bodyguard or hit man type. Well it was getting to be four thirty and we needed some dope. The best place to go was Parring Parkway, also known as the strip. The trick was to make contact without running into a NARC (narcotics police).

Well there we were cruising along when we spotted our first contact. She was hitchhiking down the strip. She looked good from the back. A nice tight ass in short shorts, long black hair and a pair of tits that really complimented the rest of her body. We pulled over to the side of the highway about twenty feet in front of her and stopped. She began running towards us with those tits just jumping in the breeze. What a sight.

Finally she approached the car and started to get into the back seat when she saw String. She stepped back and asked, "What's wrong with him". "Nothing", I said, "He just needs some juice." (Drugs).

She said, "Whoa!" closed the rear door and jumped into the front seat with me and Rabbit. She wasn't a bad looking chick but you could see the fresh track marks (needle marks) on her arms. And the teeth were really bad. All in all I wouldn't screw her with a rabbit's dick for fear it might fall off. We did a quick introduction and then got right to the point.

"Hey babe, you holding?" (Do you have any drugs?)

"No," she replied, "I just finished popping but my main man is gone. Could you guys use a blow job? Just $15 dollars for the both of you."

"I don't know", pointing to String. We laughed and said "No, Thanks, that we needed the money to get down (buy some drugs)"

It was clear she was working the strip. We went another block or so and she wanted out so we dropped her off. Makes you wonder about people like her. She was really quite pleasant and I'm sure she gave good head. It was just those rotten teeth and needle marks.

Well things weren't looking good and then we spotted another hitch hiker. We pulled up next to him and he took one look at us and said, "No thanks."

The paranoia these junkies have is unreal. We reached the end of the strip and decided to back up the other way.

Maybe our luck would change. Sure enough, as soon as we turned around there stood a fine looking young man about 22, wanting a ride. He was about 5'9, 155 pounds, and clean cut but there was something about him that made him stand out. We stopped; he ran up and jumped right into the backseat.

He was so full of life, he was bubbling over with it. He immediately introduced himself. "Hi guys, my name is Lewis, but my friends call me Lucky. How are you guys doing?"

I didn't think we would get a word in edgewise. This guy just wouldn't shut up. We finally introduced ourselves, "Rabbit, Animal and String."

"Very unique names", he replied, "And I am sure you all have the personality to match. Today must be my lucky day. I've been trying to get a ride all day. Say where are you guys headed?"

"Nowhere in particular," I replied, "We are just cruising.".

",e said. Leaning forward to the front seat he continued, "I can see there are no keys in the ignition. This must be a stolen car and I could be the man."

With this I pulled over to the side of the road, stopped, pulled out my 45 caliber automatic from my waist belt and stuck it under his chin. Grabbing him by his hair, I asked him, "Who the fuck are you? Are you the man? Cuz I will blow your shit away right now."

"No, no, please, I was just stating a point," he said. With this he says, "How do I not know that you aren't the man?" Just then String who had little to say jumped forward on the front seat and squealed out, "Shoot the motherfucker!"

Then Rabbit joined in, "Take the cocksucker out.".

The kids face turned pale white. I do believe he pissed himself as I cocked the hammer on my pistol. "No guys, please listen." "I can help you. Remember, I am Lucky Lewis."

Well I'm sure at this point we appeared to be three of the craziest fuckers that he had ever me.

As I pushed him into the back seat. Lucky said, "You're cool as far as I'm concerned. I just escaped from the correction facility....I've been out now for five days....I've had some good luck. The first day I ripped off my grandmothers' house and stole her jewelry and money...then I got into a crap game and lost everything after which time they beat me up...bad luck. But now I run into you guys."

I was tired of listening to his blubbering and told him to shut the fuck up. We cruised a little further down the strip when I said to Rabbit, "Man, we have to get down (get some drugs)."

Well this kid jumped up like he was hit in the ass with a needle and started to talk fast. I had to tell him to slow down. "I can get you some shit, he said."

"Well now we're getting somewhere, I replied." Lucky Lewis started to give us directions to his supplier. It was about four blocks off the strip. We pulled up to a house at 132 Court Street.

I pulled out a twenty dollar bill and handed it to String. "You go with him so he doesn't rip us off...You got a problem with that Lucky?"

"No, that's cool, he replied. Well String and Lucky approached and knocked on the front door. The porch light came on because it was getting dark. A curtain moved from the window...Lucky approached and the front door opened. Lucky and String weren't gone five minutes when they came back to the car. String looked at me and started to grin from ear to ear showing me his bad teeth. As he opened his hand he revealed two nickel bags (five dollar bags) of smack (heroin). Well now it was time to congratulate Lucky.

I turned around in my seat and faced Lucky. I said, "You're okay dude, sorry if I rattled your cage earlier."

Lucky replied, "Well, shit happens sometimes," and gave me a thumbs up.

Then Rabbit said, "That's not enough for all of us."

"Well," I said, "First, we have to think about...." and before I finished my statement Rabbit said, "Needles... How are we going to fire up without?"

"Needles? Have no fear, I can do that," said Lucky. I started to get a warm feeling inside. I felt good all over. Lucky Lewis couldn't do enough for us and I was glad to have him along. Following his directions Lucky took us to 23 S. Speaker Court. It was a classy neighborhood. This time I let Rabbit go with Lucky and my twenty dollar bill. It was really a nice looking house. It was made of brick and you could see that a gardener took good care of the place. Rabbit and Lucky disappeared up the long walkway to the house. The whole deal took about ten minutes.

When Rabbit and Lucky returned to the car they were accompanied by a tall blonde long haired man. Lucky introduced the guy saying, "Guys, this is Mickey, my friend. His dad is a doctor and he got us this." He then handed me a brown paper bag and I opened it to find five syringes with needles.

Mickey stated, "Lucky says you guys are cool, good people....nice car." With this said we all shook hands and Mickey disappeared up the walkway.

More and more I realized that Lucky Lewis was indeed a lucky charm for us. As we drove off into the night I stated for Lucky to hear, "We're getting low on gas and we're out of money." I could see the paranoia setting in on Lucky. He wanted to shoot up and call it a night. I knew he had a lot more to offer and I wasn't going to let this golden goose go. I quickly pulled the car over off the road in front of a store. Lucky was practically in my lap. I pulled my Colt 45 out, drew the slide to the rear and chambered a round.

I then turned to Lucky so that we were face to face and said, "I'm going to stick this fucking place up. We need money."

With this said he got very excited and grabbed my arm stating, "No man, be cool, I know where we can get some money."

I replied, "No fuck it, I can do this."

Lucky started to shout like a pleading baby for a toy, "No please, we don't want to have to kill anyone for money...we have to be cool."

String and Rabbit joined into the conversation. Rabbit stated that Lucky was right, "We have to be cool."

String on the other hand was saying, "Fuck it, do it, son of a bitch." By now if Lucky had any doubts or paranoia I quickly changed his mind. Lucky was now working overtime.

"Listen." he said, "While I was out, I stole five cars and dumped them all in the same spot."

Well I light up like a Christmas tree and blurted out, "No shit, Lucky comes through again." I stuck my pistol back into my belt feeling good about not having to stick the store up. "You know Lucky, I said, "You're a pretty cool operator. We are planning on going to California; do you want to come with us?"

"That sounds cool, he says, but first lets get these cars." Lucky started to give us the directions to the stolen cars when all of a sudden we approached the parking lot of the Union Hall workers. They must have had a meeting or something because the place was packed with cars.

All of a sudden Lucky bolted from our car and disappeared into the parking lot. I had no idea what the hell was going on. I told String and Rabbit to sit tight, that I would go look for him. My mind was racing like a freight train. What scared him off? We got the dope and needles and were headed for the stolen cars to get money. Everything was going smooth. I wondered if I overreacted and frightened him off. My heart was pumping and I started to sweat. What the hell could have happened? Suddenly I heard a tapping sound on my window. I thought for sure it was the police.

It was so dark I could hardly see that skinny figure of Lucky Lewis. In his hands he is holding about 20 tape decks that he stole from a car.

Handing me the tapes he said, "I couldn't resist...it was so easy." With this he got back into the car. We all started to laugh. This guy really put one over on us. Well we drove several miles into Baltimore County following Lucky's directions. Down a long dirt road that ended in a dead end.

Sure enough, there were five cars. Lucky started to clap his hands and stated, "I told you guys, here for the taking."

As he grinned from ear to ear I got out of the car to see if these were really popped (stolen) cars. It was clear from the broken windows and wired ignitions that these were the cars that Lucky had popped and dumped here.

It was pitch black after I turned the head lights off. I sat in the darkness as I spoke to the group. "O.K., we'll take the hubcaps for tonight just to show our fence (the person who deals in stolen goods) good faith...then we can come back tomorrow morning and really strip them clean."

Everyone agreed so we went about getting the hubcaps. We then drove down the dirt road towards the city. It had been a long and busy night. I was tired and pretty low on gas. No one said a word all the way home. I drove down Edison Highway and made my right turn into the parking lot and up the ramp. All of a sudden Lucky shouted out in the dark, "Hey this looks like the police station."

To calm him down I stated, "Where else would you get rid of hot property."

With that Lucky replied, "Man you guys are so fucking cool." With that being said the three of us, String, Rabbit and me started to whistle. That was the signal to let Lucky Lewis know he was under arrest as were all undercover narcotic officers....Lucky Lewis's luck just turned to shit.

What a night, two dope dealers...a doctors son....stolen tapes and five stolen cars not to mention an escapee from the correctional institution who was very cool, but unlucky.

Chapter Nine

Car 254

Car 254

It was a brisk day on October 15. I was walking my post called "The Harford Straightaway." The post was three blocks long and it was made up of bars, poolrooms, and hockshops. Usually when someone got stationed on this post it was because they had screwed up but I enjoyed the challenge and excitement of the post. You guessed it, I requested to work it.

Working the 4 to 12 was when you got most of the action and I was just crazy enough to love the shift. I've been with the Baltimore City Police Department for ten years now and today was a special day for me. Because the post was so busy and the fact that I worked alone on foot patrol, I was getting the chance to try out a new piece of equipment. It was a brand new Walkie Talkie. I was able to hear all the chatter between the radio cars and Headquarters. I felt like I had a side partner. If I needed help all I had to do was push a button and the radio cars usually manned by two officers would immediately be on the way to my location.

We had been trying to get money for Walkie Talkies for a long time, but we couldn't prove their value. Tonight would change all that. At about 8 p.m. I heard a radio transmission between headquarters and mobile patrol, that being the radio car. "In pursuit of Anne Arundel radio car 254 being driven by a Black male 6'4 200 lbs. He is armed and has a female hostage from Sears and Roebuck." At first I didn't think too much about the chatter because this was all happening about 50 miles from my location. As I listened I learned that the Black male had held up the Sears and Roebuck store in Anne Arundel County. The female working there hit the holdup alarm button and two county police officers responded in car 254.

When they entered Sears to see what the problem was the holdup man was waiting for them. With his gun in hand he held them at bay and took their revolvers and handcuffed them to a pole. He then took the Black female hostage and got into the police car 254 and sped away. He had two police revolvers and $5,000 in cash along with a hostage.

As I listened, I realized that this was not a normal chase pursuit. Because of the hostage, the pursuing units were simply following Car 254. He was only traveling at 25 miles per hour and heading my way. I learned that Car 254 would stop at different locations, roll the window down a few inches, and negotiate with the pursuing officers. He would take off again after each interaction.

The main concern was that he threatened to shoot the hostage if any one tried to take him. As the pursuit went on through the county roads and back into the city the number of pursuing vehicles increased. We now had a procession of about thirty police vehicles involved. We had Anne Arundel, Baltimore County, Baltimore City and the FBI all in line following this guy. It looked just like when O. J. Simpson was being pursued. My heart started to pump and I got that rush that only comes when you are in a life or death situation. Car 254 was now two miles from my location and heading straight for me. Somehow I know it was meant to be. I was going to get involved.

I started to run down the street towards the procession of units. Dodging between parked cars and running through back alleys I saw the units go by. I couldn't believe it; I actually caught up to them. The sweat was pouring off of me. My heart was pumping like a freight train. I ran alongside the string of units until I caught up to a Baltimore City unit. I banged on the window and got his attention. He pulled over long enough for me to jump in the car. I couldn't believe I had made it this far. I was like a kid at Christmas time. The officer driving the unit was a good friend of mine and when I got in the car he simply said, "Edwards what the hell are you doing?"

I responded, "I've been listening to this chase for over an hour on these new Walkie Talkies and I knew his ass was mine."

Just then Car 254 stopped at an intersection and like before he rolled down the window. He wanted to negotiate. The units following Car 254 immediately surrounded him.

The car I was in was about 25 yards from the intersection. I observed My Captain approaching Car 254 on foot and proceeded to try and negotiate with the guy.

I could hear the women screaming, "Please don't shoot me, please don't shoot me."

While the Captain was still negotiating with the guy I noticed an officer crawl under the back of Car 254 and push something into the tailpipe. The Captain was doing a good job distracting the holdup man. I then heard chatter over the radio that the officer was putting a rag into the tailpipe in an attempt to disable Car 254. Call it a premonition, but at this time I got a gut felling that things were going to turn to shit.

I told my buddy officer to give me his revolver as I drew mine from my holster. With a pistol in each hand I then told my buddy, "If the Son of a bitch shoots the Captain just ram the fucking car and I'll empty both guns into the bastard." At that split second all I could think about was my Captains' safety.

I was really wired. My palms were sweating and my chest was tight. I couldn't take my eyes off the Captain. I wanted this SOB bad. As I rolled my window down I couldn't think in the terms of what was right or wrong. I was functioning on adrenaline. This all took place in a matter of seconds. I cocked the hammers back on both pistols getting ready to unleash the hammers of hell. Just then I saw the Captain step back from Car 254 and the assailant slowly pulled away.

Wow, talk about mixed emotions. On one hand the Captain was safe, but on the other, this son of a bitch was on the move and pulling our strings like we were puppets. I managed to snap back to reality and returned my buddies pistol and re-holstered mine. Only then did I realize the consequences of my action had I pulled the triggers. Before I could chastise myself for a fucked up game plan we were on the move again.

Car 254 slowly rolled down the street .Everyone jumped back into their cars and the parade was on again. I just knew that I and the driver of Car 254 would meet again.

As we followed for about a city block I began to feel very much at ease and in total control of myself .Then it happened, Car 254 stopped at the intersection and just like before he was immediately surrounded by the police. I'm not sure what came over me but I jumped out of my buddies' police unit and ran up to the Captain. When I approached him I said, "This shit has gone on long enough. We have to stop this bastard."

Now keep in mind the Captain was not only my supervisor but we were good friends and I knew he respected my opinion. We were now just two police officers trying to deal with a nasty situation.

I felt good when he responded, "You're right we have to stop him right here." With that he pulled out a pocket knife and suggested flattening the tires.

I told him, "I'll do it." He handed me the knife and then approached the driver of Car 254 to distract him. While the captain was talking I looked around and realized we were completely surrounded by police and their weapons were drawn. If one shot was fired we would probably kill each other in the cross fire. The trick now was to get close enough to Car 254 in order to flatten the tires. I had to keep reminding myself to go slow and easy so that the hostage would not get hurt.

Car 254 was now in the center of all the police units approximately 15 yards to the closest police unit. The Captain continued to negotiate while I crawled under the back of Car 254. I could hear the women pleading with the man not to hurt her. I drove the knife into the rear tire. Nothing happened. The tires were too tough for the knife to penetrate. I decided that if that didn't work then I would let the air out of the tires. Although everything was happening very fast around me it seemed like slow motion as I was lying on the ground.

I managed to flatten two tires when I heard the Captain Say, "Enough is enough, tell us what you want for the hostage?"

The assailant replied, "Give me a cop so's I can get red of this crying bitch."

As I lay on the ground of course it started to rain. I was now cold wet and frankly had just had enough of this bullshit.

I heard the Captain reply, "No more hostages." I don't know what came over me but I decided to swap places with the female hostage. I rolled out from under the car and stood up with my hands in the air.

I was on the passenger side of Car 254 as I shouted to the driver "Ill change places with her." I didn't know what good I would be. I had left my weapon back in the Captain's car, knowing the assailant would search me.

The driver replied, "He'll do, now you get the fuck out of here." to the Captain. As the Captain returned to his vehicle I was told to strip.

Of course by this time a large crowd had gathered and stared to shout, "Give us the woman, we'll show you what to do with her."

Now there I was standing in the friggen rain starting to take off my clothes and the crowd started to chant "da da da dum da da dum ."

I might as well have been performing at a strip club. Well I got my coat off and made up my mind that I wasn't going to go any further. I raised my hands above my head and turned around for the gunman's inspection. I stood there with not a clue what to do next. It was like a circus and I was the star act.

Again everything started to happen in slow motion. I could clearly see all the police hovering behind their vehicles with their weapons drawn yet hopelessly waiting for something or someone to make the next move. I honestly had no clue about what to do next. Finally I shouted to the driver, "What are you waiting for, let's do it, her for me."

Just then the passenger door of Car 254 swung open. My mind started to click a mile a minute. In thinking what to do next, I figured the hostage would get out on the passenger side, I could grab her, fall to the ground, and my fellow officers would fill this asshole full of lead. As I was convincing myself that this was a good plan everything went to shit.

The gunmen shouted to me "Get in the car," at the same time dragging the woman across the seat and out the drivers' side of the vehicle. He had one arm around her neck as he placed his revolver into her stomach. He shouted to me "I'll kill this bitch if you don't get into the fucking car."

Realizing I had no choice I got into the passenger side of Car 254 with my hands still in the air... I left the door wide open as I sat there on the front seat trying to figure this guy out .The gunmen was still holding onto the woman   He moved from the driver's side of the car to my side and continued to move into the center of the surrounding   police cars and had nowhere to go.

Now keep in mind the unruly crowd was getting worse by the minute. They continued to shout "Give us the girl!" It seemed like everything was frozen in time. No one could make a move for fear of the hostage being shot. I sat there on the edge of the front seat half way in and half way out of Car 254.

The crowd was really getting large. Now the police were shouting, "Let the women go."

The shouting was coming from all directions. As I sat there hopelessly I looked down and saw the two police revolvers and the bag of money taken in the robbery. That's when I realized this guy had no way out. There was no way to avoid a shooting.

Then it happened, call it a life and death feeling but I knew I wasn't going to let anyone get shot or let that women get hurt. The shouting kept getting louder and louder. People all over were yelling, "Let the woman go."

Like a light bulb being turned on I saw the way out. I noticed that with all the people shouting from different directions the gunmen would move his head from left to right side to side looking at the people. The one important thing was every time he moved his head from side to side his gun hand, the hand that held his pistol into the woman's stomach, would move away from her into the direction that he was looking. I got so excited I almost pissed myself. I just knew this was going to work.

I got on Car 254's radio and told the dispatcher what I had observed and to advise all police on the scene to start shouting at the gunman. The gunman was about twenty feet from me. I made up my mind what I was going to do. The trick was to be fast enough to get between the gun and the hostage. I then heard the dispatcher relay my request and like singing in a choir all the officers started to shout, "Let that women go."

With all of the bystanders and the police yelling "Let the woman go" it was a hell of a distraction. The gunman's head would shift from right to left. I could see he was really distracted with the sweat running down his face. I could clearly see his pistol move completely away from her body. I took a deep breath

Like my ass was on fire I jumped from the front seat of Car 254 and got between the gun and the hostage. I threw my whole body into him as I grabbed his pistol and pulled down as hard as I could on his wrist. His weapon fell to the ground and fifty police stormed in on him. The screaming hostage was whisked away to safety as my fellow officers continued to whale on the gunman. Nightsticks and slapjacks were flying everywhere even managing to hit me several times in the head. I finally managed to get to my feet with the assailant in hand.

I later learned that I hit him so hard I broke his wrist and dislocated his shoulder. I don't know how long I stood there in the rain soaking wet but I soon realized that everyone was gone, even Car 254. I still had my Walkie Talkie though and I called for my police buddy to meet me and take me back to the station house.

Upon my arrival I was met by scores of news men and reporters. I was asked to tell how it all went down. Before I could say a word my Captain approached me and shook my hand. He said, "Job well done. You will get the Medal of Honor for this one." The Captain also wanted me to tell the press how this was a team effort between the different police departments.

Well, I told press what they wanted to hear.

I learned that the gunman was immediately taken into custody by the FBI. As for me I was still wet and had a splitting headache as I returned home. The next day the headlines in the newspaper's read "Hostage maintains her cool under duress." As the weeks went by I received many awards from the Governor, the Mayor and Congressmen. I even received a Letter of Commendation from the Vice President of the United States, Spiro Agnew. I also received The Medal of Honor.

After all was said and done all I could remember was when I returned home that night as I put my key into the door lock for some strange reason my hand started to tremble uncontrollably. I had a terrible empty feeling in my stomach. I knew I had cheated death one more time.

Chapter Ten

Clean Sweep

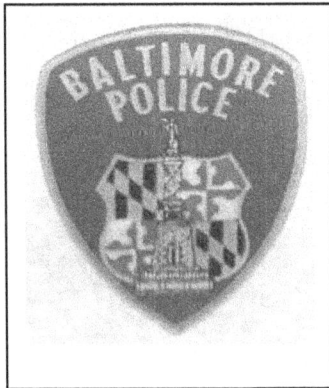

Clean Sweep

It was a crisp day in October. Just cold enough to wear a coat. I was walking my old post 319 assigned to the Harford Road straight away.

I saw a Black women sitting on the front steps of a house. She wasn't wearing a coat but she didn't seem to be cold. She appeared to have been crying. I said "Hello" to her and she responded "Hi."

It was now about midnight and it just seemed a little odd for this woman to be out alone. I asked her name and she replied "Janet Jefferson."

"Are you okay?" I asked.

In a very soft voice she muttered, "Yes I'm fine."

I said, "Ok," in a cheerful manner and continued to walk down the street. There was definitely something wrong. Walking about a half a block I still couldn't get her out of my mind. I turned around to walk back to were the Black female was. Reaching the house I found the front door open and she was gone. I called several times with no response.

I just had a gut feeling something was wrong. Turning my flashlight on, my suspicions were confirmed. I observed a large thick pool of blood in the front doorway. As I entered the house it got a lot worse. There was blood everywhere, smeared on the walls, and on the steps going up the stairs. I never saw so much blood. I drew my revolver and continued to slowly walk up the blood soaked steps. I was being very careful not to disturb the crime scene.

I worked my way up the winding stairs. The house was very hot .I started to sweat, my eyes were shifting everywhere back and forth. All I could see was pools of smeared blood. The silence was broken by the beat of my heart. I wanted to take in a breath of fresh air. The heat started to become very uncomfortable. I unbuttoned my jacket and moved my flashlight in quick jerks from left to right. The place was filthy dirty. Pots and pans were everywhere. I thought, *My god where did all this blood come from*? The heat started to make me nauseous. I shined my light on what appeared to be a pile of rags. That's when I found him. What was left of a Black male .He had been sliced open multiple times. His fingers and hands were just barely hanging there. They were injuries probably suffered when he tried to grab the ten inch butcher knife now sticking out of his face.

The odor from the house was now getting to me. I found a light switch but it didn't work. I had to get out of there. My breathing was rapid and when I turned to leave I bumped smack into the Black female standing in the dark. I was so stunned I dropped my flashlight. I almost pissed myself.

In shear panic I started to shout "Don't move this is the police." I must have said that four times while scrambling for my flashlight. She just scared the living shit out of me. My flashlight rolled into a pool of blood but I could care less. I picked it up and headed for the front door. I ran down the creaking steps. All I wanted was to get outside.

Once I got outside the house I felt like a hundred pound weight had been lifted off my chest. Quickly I sucked in the fresh brisk night air.

Waiting a few moments to gain my composure I called out, "Miss Jefferson, Come on out, it's okay. It's the police."

Very slowly she appeared in the doorway. In a soft voice she muttered "He was with another woman so I killed him." She appeared to be in shock. I kind of felt sorry for her. After placing handcuffs on this three hundred pound woman I told her she was under arrest. All the time I waited for the homicide squad to arrive she just stared into space. Of all the people to show up for the homicide squad it was my old partner and friend Willy

Boyd. I was glad to turn everything over to Willy and left the area. It was now about one thirty in the morning.

My post was starting to shut down. The pool halls were closed. Same for the pawn shops. The bars closed at two. I had time to make one good round and check each bar before two o'clock. I really never had much trouble from the bars on my post except for one bar, a place called The Cassasa Club. It was a breeding place for trouble. A lot of prostitution and drugs deals there. I would get at least one shooting or stabbing every two weeks from there. I couldn't get close enough to anything in order to close the place down. The clientele hated police. The owner in particular hated police especially White police.

On one particular rainy day in the past I had walked into the crowded bar with my rain coat on. I walked from the front door to the back door making my way through the crowd .After getting outside I found that someone had sliced the back of my rain coat open with what appeared to be a straight razor. I knew who was doing what in the bar but I just couldn't get close enough to make an arrest.

Everyone would cover for each other. Take "Bunny" for instance. I knew he was the biggest drug dealer on my post, but I couldn't catch him. They didn't call him Bunny for nothing. He would actually taunt me and then dare me to catch him. Always staying about ten feet away from me. Well tonight was a treat as I approached the street corner where the Club Cassasa was located.

The club was empty as so was the house next door to it. The abandoned house next door to the Cassasa was where junkies would go to shoot up their drugs. It was now past two o'clock in the morning and all the bars were supposed to be empty of patrons so I figured why not drop in on Mister Congeniality. Well I opened the front door and to my surprise I saw he had one customer after hours. And guess who it was. Yes, thank you God, it was Bunny. He was backed into a corner between me and the bar. I knew I had to act quickly. My gut told me that he was holding drugs somewhere on his person.

I immediately reached for him and grabbed him by the collar and told him he was under arrest. He reached into his pants pocket and pulled out a wad of money and handed it to the bar owner. He said, "Take this so the pig can't get it."

We started to struggle, the bar owner grabbed the drug money and put it into the cash register. I had my hands full with Bunny. We started to roll around on the floor. Not knowing what the bar owner would do next. I called on my Walkie Talkie, "10-13 "assist an officer, and my location. Within minutes uniform police were pouring through the front door. We got Bunny restrained and handcuffed him from behind. Well it gets better. After everything was under control and all the uniform guys were there I placed the bar owner under arrest for obstruction of justice. He was fuming and calling me one name after another. So I felt it only fair to take his liquor license off the wall and confiscate it. Then I opened the cash register and took all of the money. Seeing as how I couldn't tell what was the drug money I took all of it and tagged it as evidence. All 600 dollars.

Now I finally got the bar owner and the liquor license which would shut down the bar for ninety days and I had Bunny. We got to the police station and I placed Bunny in a small room and told him to strip. He didn't like it a little bit. He asked me where my probable cause was. Well this time I was ready. While working the tactical unit I learned all about probable cause. So I let him have it. I told him that I had received information from a CI saying that a subject named Bunny wearing clothes fitting his description was in the Cassasa bar at two o'clock in the morning dealing drugs and that he would have drugs in his possession.

Of course that was a lot of shit. But seeing as how I didn't have to name my CI source it would hold up in court. This helps when you get that gut feeling and need probable cause. If I was wrong I would simply apologize and cut him loose. But I knew I was right. Well he started to strip and after taking off each piece of clothing he would throw it onto a pile.

I approached the pile and started to go through his clothes when he grabbed the cheeks of his ass and spread them apart shouting, "Here check my ass."

Then came that gut feeling. He really didn't want me to go through his clothes. I put on a pair of rubber gloves and picked up his underwear. Sure enough just in front of the fly was a little pocket and in that little pocket contained twenty bags of heroin. My gut feeling had paid off. I finely had Bunny. I finished my paperwork and returned to my post. It was now four o'clock in the morning. I was at the far end of my post about three blocks away when I heard the sirens from the fire engines. I walked briskly to the place of the fire.

It seemed that a person or persons unknown had set the abandoned house and the Club Cassasa on fire. It was quite a blaze. It burned both buildings down to the ground. The Fire Marshal arrived and it turned out that he was an old friend of mine. I told him what had happen that night and how the bar owner felt about police. Well he told me the fire was arson and nobody would get a nickel of insurance until the case was solved. Now I'm going to get on that case tomorrow or maybe the next day. Anyway you look at it was a clean sweep. I solved a homicide, got rid of Bunny, got rid of a rats nest, that being the bar and a crack house.

It was a good night's work!

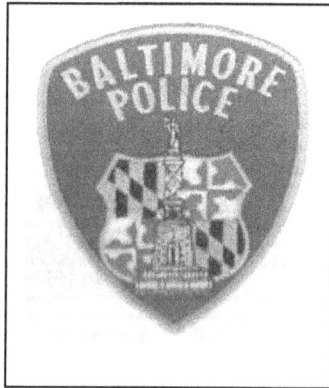

The End

www.ingramcontent.com/pod-product-compliance
Lightning Source LLC
LaVergne TN
LVHW011359080426
835511LV00005B/350